Keep Calm I Have A Spreadsheet for That

www.ingramcontent.com/pod-product-compliance
Lightning Source LLC
Chambersburg PA
CBHW070430220526
45466CB00004B/1609
9781658317092